MOVING &
ST RAGE

MOVING &
ST RAGE

Kathy Fagan

Winner, Vassar Miller Prize in Poetry,
T. R. Hummer, Judge

University of North Texas Press
Denton, Texas

Printed in the United States of America.
First edition 1999
5 4 3 2 1

Permissions:
University of North Texas Press
PO Box 311336
Denton TX 76203-1336
940-565-2142

The paper used in this book meets the minimum requirements of the American National Standard for Permanence of Paper for Printed Library Materials, z39.48.1984. Binding materials have been chosen for durability.

Library of Congress Cataloging-in-Publication Data

Fagan, Kathy.
    MOVING & ST RAGE / by Kathy Fagan.
        p.   cm.
    ISBN 1–57441–066–0 (paper : alk. paper)
    I. Title.   II. Title: MOVING & ST RAGE.
PS3556.A326M68   1999
811'.54--dc21   98–45421
                                CIP

Design by Angela Schmitt
Cover image courtesy of the Rare Books and Manuscripts Division
of the Ohio State University Libraries.

Acknowledgments

Grateful acknowledgment is made to the editors of the following magazines for printing these poems: *Agni* ("MOVING & ST RAGE"), *The Antioch Review* ("To a Reader"), *Barrow Street* ("*Her Meditation on the Subject of Universal Phenomena*"), *Denver Quarterly* ("Lacuna, Lacustrine"), *The Kenyon Review* ("Driving It" & "Sign"), *Michigan Quarterly Review* ("*She Attempts to Tell the Truth About True Romance*"), *The Missouri Review* ("Revisionary Instruments," "Triptych," "Altitude," "Vigil," and "Easter Sunday"), *The New Republic* ("Portrait of a Girl as the Letter A"), *New Virginia Review* ("Blue"), *The Paris Review* ("There Are Plenty of Angels, *She Said in the LADIES*," "California, *She Replied*," & "*Her Advice to the Still Life Painter*"), *Ploughshares* ("Two Tragedies, with Preface"), *Shenandoah* ("Grief"), and *Southwest Review* ("A Vocabulary of Icons").

"Solstice" first appeared in *Under 35: The New Generation of American Poets* (Anchor/Doubleday, 1989, edited by Nicholas Christopher) and *Mountain Intervals: Poems from The Frost Place* (Meriden-Stinehour Press, 1987, edited by Donald Sheehan). "The End of the Story" first appeared in *Piecework: 19 Fresno Poets* (Silver Skates, 1987, edited by Ernesto Trejo & Jon Veinberg).

My thanks to the Ingram Merrill Foundation and The National Endowment for the Arts for grants which supported the completion of this book. Gratitude also goes to The Frost Place, The Corporation of Yaddo, and, especially, The MacDowell Colony for residencies that allowed me to write many of these poems. To Scott Cairns and Terry Hummer, to Stuart Lishan, Janie Fink, and Mike White, and to the friends, colleagues, and mentors who helped shape this book over the years, my endless thanks. And to A . . . .

For Jackie
1947–1991

Contents

Portrait of a Girl as the Letter A

As in -line or -frame.
As in alpha, angel,
Arms of a merciful Jesus

Extended. As in clockhands
Signing 7:25, compass
On point, cloak rounding

A corner. It's summer
Where she is and she's angry
There. As in feet spread

Apart and planted for the camera,
Sleeveless skin peeling
Like eucalyptus bark

In light the color of eucalyptus:
Time dried to a powder.
She is the only angular thing

On the planet. Her body,
A brand on it: scissor, wedge,
Tent opened on

A hill's ascent; the horizon,
Her bar horizontal.
The beauty of architecture is

In the standing. As in ox
In its yoke, as in
Ace played, lancet

Arch, little bird
With folded wings
Waiting. Look at her there

So like herself! The sky
Is a room behind her, and she,
The article in it, the letter of

The name she stands for.

Sign

He said he liked the slouch & lean of it, the Dietrich Garbo
Dean & Brando up against the wall of it in both my hand
& his. He had a fondness for Russian novels, my boy-
Friend. He stuttered a little. He said he
Liked the throat of it, the fat of tongue,
Back of palate, wind-up, pitch & hock-
A-lugie charm of it. He tracked
Animals on weekends, that boy-
Friend. Ejaculated pre-
Maturely. Fork &
Absence is what
I thought.
Stuck
Arrowhead.
Left margin.
This X doesn't do
Subjunctive, doesn't
Care to equal much of any-
Body's anything. Nobody's variable.
Nobody's mark. Just its own gold butterfly
Flying hurriedly west (O don't rush so lest your
Wings shred like pennants like ribbons like lines!).
Around 1000 B.C., Phoenicians gave their letter K the name
Kaph—what babies call me: kaph—which means "hollow of the hand."

Lacuna, Lacustrine

The lake has a hold in it
is what the child says
The lake has a hold in it where the fish jump through
by which she means
when like a needle then a fish does jump
bite and dive
lake filling where the body was and closing in on its return
just as the fish's mouth had shut
round something that we could not see
(but faster, imperceptibly)
by which the child means
waving now
because the wind is up and cold
and we've turned back
and fog has muffled even the gulls' cries
hammered as they've been this while to sky above the lake
by which she means
the child
waving now
hold most emphatically and not goodbye
palm cupped in
the Italian way
in a gesture of possession
because the hand has not yet learned to turn outward

A Vocabulary of Icons

Like the memory of any childhood—
all talk and render.
Speculation. Allegory.
Jesus, of course, and the dark
horse, bleating lamb, scapegoat-

gods who must die so
quickly—a lunar beauty in the blood
sacrifice. As for
wallpaper, then, we shall choose
roses. And let

the drapes be white and sheer
and billow lightly
in every season. Mother—
one should be there—
looks happy over her copper cookware.

And children playing catch in the street
before supper—
I think it is a field they play in
as the sun sets—
are never cold, never strange.

You'd have to spit
in a hanky to clean the kisses from their cheeks.
You'd have to carry them in
in your own strong arms.
For she'd said carnations

and presented them with her mouth.
She'd whispered snow
then brought it with her hands.
On this experts concur:
that only by woman

can the thing be lured and captured,
and by man will be exhibited
in the palace of the king
whose floors are like ice
that permit no passage.

Elemental

like light
or dust
like lit dust around
a doorframe
like vermin or water pressing
round that door
like oil or smoke or voices
like a strong
smell yes
an odor
like winter like hiding like
stories with their edges
glowing
not gilded no
but the glow before
the page burns black
that line where the fire
is and was and is again
that glissade
like lightning
a city come upon
after dark
that petal fold
the peeling a blossom does
until it is not
a blossom
blown they call it
up in smoke yes
light pressing inward
from the brief burn

then out
that it's both at once
the racing toward
away
a living thing they call it
for its breath I think
for that center which is not
the center but a door
or the movement through it
from which
toward which
around
and for its odor
and for its carriage on the draft
and for the cinders that will visit
what is spared
and what is chosen that
dust that door that
light

Altitude

When smoke rose from the swung censer
       it rose on a choral breath
It rose slowly and in waves
       like the congregants   and rode
From vault to vault the nave's
       ceiling   where   we believed
It found escape
       We believed in transcendence then
As we believe in movies   each Christmas
       and from the very first   reel
That even the smallest prayer may pass
       through nebulaic dust to heaven
Where the ratio of angel   to living man
       is one to one
Believed as we believe in dreams
       pinned to spots of light above us
And in actions finding answer
       in an out of reach   elsewhere
Believed with the belief that drops the "t"
       from constellation   when looking toward
The stars   Desire is its own pilot
       at this or any season   traversing the city
And clouds lit by the city   the illumined
       cloudcover like a landscape
Transposed   a language made legible
       on buoyant tongues   It is not a trick
Of fuel tailings or engine's din   but a visible
       sheen   an audible innocence
In which the lights of approach and departure
       seem one   And as a season's

Rain ticks at our tablet windows
  a mechanization of gears in the belly
Goes round like applause
  among passengers at touchdown

Chronology of March

Then all at once the future was foretold,
   and told for good as it had to be.
Nothing could be left to chance, you see,

   and who, in truth, has preferred otherwise?
Tell us a story, the children demanded,
   and none was denied them.

For lovely are the gizmos, the easy
   folds of order, the shapeliness arisen
From a need fulfilled. And blessed, therefore,

   is misery, explicable and common-
Place, a bit in the mouth we savor and chew
   on and do not resist, can not think to

       2.

   resist. In March, for instance,
Before the worm-moon shakes its bottom from
   a pail of blue, and seed packets appear

Too early in the stores—those envelope
   maracas, that High Mass of names:
Cosmos   Coreopsis   Delphinium—

   and the dome of heaven gets
Festooned with stars, with stars and wreaths of stars
   as it is in winter,

It's then, briefly, there's burn at the trueness of things,
 a tug, an edge, of essential hunger seen:
Fiery raiment! Look not upon it lest thine eyes. . . .

3.

When the wild dogs of our county, starved
 once in like weather, started pulling
Bodies from the vet's pit, he had to begin
 burning them every day. There'd been of course

The public outcry, the health hazard and
 unseemliness of it all, but what disturbed
The doctor most was how the pack was dying
 of the lime he'd spread—though at a distance, freshly

Cast, it seemed even to him sometimes
 to look like snow. Spring, naturally, followed.
Corpses contaminated the water supply
 for several months. The doctor retired but refused

To move away. It's said the trees beside
 his house have not yet relaxed their huddled
Attitudes, that honey locusts there
 bear only teeth, and grow tall for the thorns,

4.

 thorns and crowns of thorns. It's true, winters are
Hard here. The white-tail who survive them feed
 mornings in our human graveyard. One sees them

Bent above the markers as if reading:
 a stone that's called FATE, a stone that says RIDDLE,
A stone that reads TRACE, first name FIDELIA.

Their very bodies will away the season,
Rounds of grass and spongy mosses rising
    where their hooves have been, their heat—

Little easters on the wheel we make:
    And they said among themselves, who
Shall roll us away the stone from the door of the sepulchre?

    Something in them knows the story,
The same in nature as in history or love,
    dragging out the dead things to make a meal of.

To a Reader

What if I did not begin as I
used to? Here is the house
and its family, I said once;
here the bride, the grave,
and the window (*oh won't you . . .*).
What if loss and desire
were not a split curtain
ever parted and joined,
and the book never opened
to a leaf you had pressed there,
and I refused all
irony, which is,
of course, accommodation?

Yesterday three deer burst
out of the field I walked in—
a fine rain, snowcover,
mist that rose from the melting—
and though I know I was
meant to forget I
remembered not you most wholly
when the smallest one of them,
spotting me, stopped, bolted,
stopped again, spun round;
and since then assuredly
a choice had been made,
resumed its place in the vanishing.

Millefleurs

Cornflowers for the hounds' eyes,
    For theirs are the eyes of the Daughters of God,
And a Virtue requires keenness of vision,
    And clarity—the very word blown from Gabriel's horn—
For the hunt. For winter has ended,

    And incarnation is a favorite topic. Carnations themselves are
The flowers of God. Nail flowers, Germans call them,
    For their clove scent and blood
Color. Everything red will be
    Read as Christ's blood. Christ's or someone else's

Blood. A pregnant woman with a choice
    Of either will be drawn
To the rose if she carries a girl, the lily for a son.
    I've played a similar game myself, involving needles
Swung from a thread,

    And there's another, involving other
Needles. Pomegranate, pimpernel . . .
    The rose we grew once
To the size of my face: that was surely a sign
    Of endurance. Periwinkle means grace. Campion,

Evil. The palm and phoenix rise up from
    The same generic name. But with their quarry ahead, why
Do the two hounds glance backward?
    A clutch of cornflowers by the road to your house
Reminded me

How they'd been set
There, five centuries ago and on another continent,
  By a designer and weaver unknown to us now.
I like to think of them as Truth and Mercy:
  Truth in the lead with her strong head,

Mercy thinner, more reluctant.
  The flowers around them look pressed
To the field. They're stitched
  To show their faces, as in the sun the pansy will—
The flower named for thought, *pensee*, or

  Love-in-idleness. Love's casualty, really.
In an unrelated portrait, *De quoilque non vede yo my recorde*
  Has been sewn onto the collar of the Lady's dress.
The thought being:
  I remember that one whom I no longer see.

MOVING & ST RAGE
—billboard on Ohio State Route 36

              Of course, something is missing,
which accounts for his sainthood, his legendary fury;
and while it would be false to say that Moving never dwelt
upon the source of that absence,
wondering what hand of god or man,
what rupture or obscuring force
might snatch a vowel from its rightful place,
              shaping him thus, charting forever
the course of their merged destinies,
equally false would be to claim
she'd loved him any other way,
or that she was not drawn to Rage
as to the flame, and he to the sentiment
her name made: his lips mouthed roundly on her
              first syllable, his jaw clenched
shut as he uttered the last; nor was the paradox lost
on them, susceptible as they were to words,
and symbols, like the ampersand,
cousin to the treble clef,
whose plainer features also set
the pitch and tumble of mortal endeavor,
              and joined these two like ones before
who'd met on the grassy medians of myth
to pledge those troths the gods grow jealous of:
there are limits placed on endless love.

And that is why Rage came to travel, and walks
the foreign seacoast of an ancient city now,
anonymous among the crowds, and through a speech so vastly
              strange, it does not interrupt his reverie;

nothing can: not the whirl of birds and white
umbrellas in the sun of the *platia*, not the darkly pretty twining couples
espaliering ocher walls—all's to Rage
a froth and sway he cannot comprehend;
and useless as it is to question
which of them felt banished first, or when
                                    their hardening of hearts began
like the fortification of separate kingdoms,
question they must, Rage & Moving, cursed to live
beyond their primes, and one half-day and -world apart,
to ride a wheel of common failures
that is hope turning up
and regret coming down, and that makes a sound like
                    See Me   See Me,
spewing grit and salt and stars, grinding
on its dark axis—and while she knows that Earth
itself has blocked the moon she loves from sight,
Moving can't recall tonight the reason
bodies spin this way, or who first named the blank
moon New, believed an unlit promise with a faith
                    the there-not-there was whole,

and not a lost and gone forever, hugely missed and missing O.

Driving It

By then it was late
Spring, and the medians and berms had that

Morning-after look about them: weedy, unshaven, vaguely
Obscene. Anyone could see

What a good drunk it had been.
It was all that green,

For one thing, set off by how the sprung
Confetti of dogwood clung

To the woods' edge, and how the birches stuck and glinted,
A quiver of bolts Neptune might have shot

Off, showing off. The sky too was turning opal—
Forerunner of summer's usual

Milk—and like the stone its heart seemed shattered,
As if it were

At fault for snow
Cottonwoods in fact had made, letting their seedpods go.

I'd been driving. The bridge was out ahead.
No—the bridge ahead

Was under construction,
Traffic slow. We'd gotten

Used to it, inured:
The word

Itself a streak
On glass. So while the roadkill of the week

Before disturbed us, while it remained,
Uncannily, what it once had been—

Despite the neon
Orange X spraypainted on

Its back—we kept driving, stop-and-going,
And heard the river echoing

The drill when the drill quit.
Years ago, in Texas, my friend took us to visit

Austin's landmark,
Treaty Oak.

The tree had been poisoned—enormous,
Imploding, it looked, she said, like a house

Plant dying—and when I asked, rhetorically, *Who would
Do a thing like that*, shaking my head,

Someone like God,
Was what my friend said.

You see I drove that road every day. I didn't want to stop
Driving it. Someone blows up

A building, someone guts his muzzled pet,
Someone beats a child to death

And it's just more news
(And not) that loses

(And not) its horror by degrees. She's dead now, she
Was dying then. We didn't want to be

Used to it, but the bridge was
Out ahead, the sky was strange with snow. And there was

Something else as well, something almost delicate
In the arrangement of the corpse around the worksite.

Someone must have used his hands: the displays
Were too calculated to be achieved otherwise,

And anyone could see what a good
Job had been done. I drove that road

Every day. I didn't mind
The wait. I liked the treeline,

The undeveloped fields, the way, that time of year,
A cardinal said *Here I*
          Here I
          Here I   am am am am am am am,
Claiming he was everywhere,

That every place was his,
And every thing. Or that it would be. Even this.

Grief

There is a bell inside this sadness
    and a hand that rings it.
There is a schoolyard of children
    lining up by their size.
And make no mistake—
    as they tumble and queue,
    as they march and file brownly
    through the doors of their rooms—
it's relief you feel now
    that the neighborhood's silent
    and the drivers relax their hands on the wheel;
relief for the jumpers and twirlers and shouters,
    for those who played,
    and who played at playing,
    and for those who watched, walking laps at the fence—
how liable, they seemed,
    to just float away,
    like the spinning wings on winter trees that stay attached
    for the time you watch them.
It's good that they're warming their desks again—
    such cold little desks
    screwed down to the floor.
And good and familiar how sleepy they feel,
    to know what they know,
    believe what they do:
that the teacher will push
    her hair from her face,
that those busses will idle like the clock on the wall—
    up   up   down   down—

and the thick brown shoes they've kept tied all day
　　will take them home,
　　where you lived once,
which is also fastened firmly to the earth.

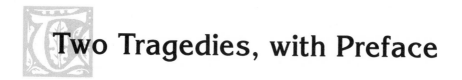Two Tragedies, with Preface

Every dusk there gather in the trees
birds whose bodies lean heavy as
magnolias on the bent and swaying branches.

Every dusk, in trees, birds gather,
looking heavy as magnolias or
the shadows of magnolias, since in color

birds are darker; and since they scatter, turning
to reassemble on their branches, burning
slowly in their song, they are, this evening,

the ashes of magnolias, and in every
way an utter fiction like the very
one I tell you now:

*

Imagine a married
couple on a weekend at the sea—
long-married people, not unfriendly

with each other. Let us picture them
smiling, even when rain hems
the details of their bodies from

our sight, and lays on everything a greyness,
false as coals concealing light. Now suppose
our husband, as his wife unpacks, sees

shadowed on the darkening sea a skiff
capsized, and figures in the waves as if
his watching put them there, and made his life

and his green eyes the truest water
into which they sank. He doesn't wonder
what to do, nor can he think to answer

when she asks, "What? What is it, hon?"
Before a word forms in his throat, he's gone.
And she, drawn slowly toward the window then

(the dream-like steps, her bridal stride!),
arrives in time to watch him join, side-
by-side, a line of men; their lengthening braid,

the only seam, now stretching, thinly, in
the swath of storm. The tiny boat they strain
to reach is lifted once and pitched again,

before two bodies drift to view, and swell
above the roiling tide. A smallish girl
is pulled to shore; a sodden dog, that's paddled

to the beach, shakes off his coat, sniffs at
the child; and then—it's over. The rain gives out.
The ocean soothes. The girl, beneath her blanket,

moves. And under others lie her parents—
still. Someone's called an ambulance.
The rest wait, shuffling, on the sand.

Suppose our husband turns to face the window
then. Or that his wife has met him down below.
Or that our lifeless parents rise to go,

holding their grateful child between them. Say
the words could make it so; and that our wife has always
loved her husband, loves him even more today.

Imagine hope there, burning through the grey,
turning like the light of the ambulance
that takes the girl away.

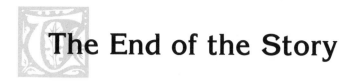

The End of the Story

When there is an end to it
and the page leans ghostly toward the bent light
when there is an end
to the storm and the night and the one hope left
there is no end
but a procession of mourners
who walk in black clothes an invisible path
between promise and intention
the shore and their homes
How can we follow to the very end
from the day of their sorrow to the day of recovery
their swift return
to what they were before
The day is the same
and the season unknowable
It could be the beginning or the end of winter
in that space revealed between snow and soil
ours to read like all good words
and with eyes to travel unintelligible maps

Easter Sunday

Church bells, rain, deer
    pellets in the pine
beds, and lichens ecstatic

    for a northern god. All morning
I have waited for a sign
    greater than these: companion

blood, an animate spirit. The body
    of a nuthatch found on my doorstep only
strengthened that need. How light

    it was! A no-weight in my hand,
as hers had been. Then too
    I waited. Believed I would have

gone where she was going
    for a sign. There are at least two
sides of grief: on one,

    you're watchful; the other makes you
turn away. And maybe we don't
    get to choose. Like at the all-you-can-

eat salad bar, the ones whose mothers didn't,
    my friend said, love
them enough, first plates piled

too high, I looked everywhere:
shadow at my left shoulder, shadow
   on my right. Then mourning

doves on the car-hood. Enclosed
   parking garage. I convinced myself
with that. But what of?

   Winter fog in the valley, summer
fog on its grape; and the lightning of spring lanced
   in fall's halved tomato.

I once dreamed a city divided
   by water. No bridge, no boat, no way across
that I could find. And the dream-

   self asked, How will the children
go to school? And her voice answered, surprising
   me, answered, Zero Street,

then said no more. Zero,
   as in nothing, as in bottom, as in
no-place-you-know

   open   closed   whole   gone.
As in open. As in whole.
   Leaves young beeches hold all winter

strike low flames through the woods
   like chandeliers lit and waiting
to be raised. It is April,

   and snow unthawed in the darker reaches
heaves as though someone breathed
   beneath it. Three days ago, sun,

and the tap, tap of creepers
　　round the base of a pine tree. That morning,
they made all the circles they wanted.

# Vigil

He was saying how any note struck on the piano that day
    even in error
was enunciated like a syllable from the perfect throat

how a moth applauds smallest
    it prays otherwise

and the saw-whet calls for who
    knows how many nights before
then feeling no need
    it does not call

    like a wick that waits for its flame to come
        (don't make me lonely)
    like a mirror waiting for its face

But I was silt on the lakebed that night
    and she the boat spun on its surface
and though it was already much too dark
    I'll wait for you here was what she said

Here and elsewhere
Her and not

Like a singular crow
    and the pine limb it sits on
        swaying perhaps

Or perhaps it was a tree entire
    conversed with the wind
        that moved it

And then someone mentioned new theory on purpose
It was the theory of original sin
    and had been
    for some millenia

    powerlines down
    hoses unmanned
and up from the loam
some runners in red
a runner and red leaves
of what

    Currents and currents and leaping
    connections
    all meaning the same as
                (don't make me)
                    lonesome

As a girl I called the hydrangea
    hi danger: powdered old women in fragrant green coats
And grandmother used the words
    far head for forehead
And of course there's always
    euthanasia

    Don't do it my friend said
    There's no hope in that

It's not prayer otherwise
    neither prayer nor piano

All that can fly you see
    strictly forbidden

Also anything that does not
    fly

Nothing but empty
vesseling there

And we need someone (my flame, my face)
      to take it in (don't make me wait)
to take it up and pour it out (I will for you here)
      again and again

an alphabet sung
to the pleasure of the child
      for the pleasure of the lesson
            and listener

Solstice

There was a sound of grouse from the field
    of grouse or a box guitar
And the way the storm idled over the mountain
    revealing the mountain   dissolving in light
Was the way the grouse and the rubbery strumming
    advanced and withdrew across the field
Crossing it thereby   not on the wind
    but on the driest memory of their own first making
And that is why fireflies startled from place
    from their daytime places in the weeds and grass
Resembled the words of a child's Vocabulary
    their lessons divulged   their lessons concealed
And to the child for whom a word yields meaning
    one word that emerges apart from its fellows
To unroll its syllables   suddenly   everywhere
    it is repetition that implies urgency
And urgent repetition that doubts it away
    like the triad of firefly beats on a screen
Green as the sliver of lime in a glass
    that lit the ice   that lit the lamp
By which the dark seemed gladly dazzled
    sure as it was of some enormity of its own
Elsewhere   and not far   from here

# Blue

The sky is breathing birds this evening,
breathing them in and out of the light.
From light to darkness, the breath of them rises,
the breath of them falls, the breasts of them glowing
where the sun is.

A sunset lasts where land is flattest.
Where can it hide?

But the needle in the flame
and the skin it's burned for—
beneath them is a hidden fire:
pilot light, blue and bluer,
like sky before the sun gets in,
like blood in our veins before the needle.

Make straight in the desert a highway for our God . . .
and watch from it the sun on either side:
needle in the gas flame, sacred heart of the pilot light.

On this side, dusk, a pink
horizon, the amethyst it gets
to be; and leafless trees—
plain as sparrow feathers here—
are startled into light, like converts
or the damned.

I wanted to be Paolo *and* Francesca.
Not one or the other but the passion between them:
    sparrow, sycamore, jumbo jetliner—
what rises and sustains its rising, a lit thing
    in remotest blue, shining in a blue
that never listens.

    Flying in God's face, is what they said.
But if not there, O pilot light,
    where then will

you fly? With the weightless dead
    at the end of the world?

I've read that on All Hallow's Eve
    the line between life and death
is thinnest. Like this horizon here:
    Make straight in the desert a needle and follow . . .

It's not the end of the world I'm thinking of
    but the other side:
the sky vein-blue and deaf still,
    not a bird in it, not a breath.
It will be morning there but not yet.
    I will be rising there but not yet.
For now, the sunset lasts and lasts,
    and there are, besides me, people watching.

Revisionary Instruments   I

Sallie sits beside me as we wait for you and studies the painting of the hot-air balloon.

From brown hills cradling blue water it rises, toward a cropped, enormous yellow sun.

I have seen it for days, this bad painting. It is remarkable only for its size, the tenacity of its brightness, and the signatures of those patients to whom it is dedicated.

I had thought I'd committed each one of them to heart.

But today I notice, suspended in middle air between the sea's horizon and basket's base, identical surnames in childish hands. One boy, one girl, their Latin name written as high as their arms could reach.

I'll remember it, later, as *Esperanza*. I'll think it impossible even as I do.

What revisionary instruments our hearts are, I'll write; *how merciful our misremembrance*,

since, if truth were known, a family of headstones was what I thought of then, floating in that patch of sky, and not of hope, not of hope at all.

California, *She Replied*

It's driving into all that goldness makes
You blind, *she said*. The road oats, timothy,
The mustard hung beside the highway like
So many crowns thrown out, *she said*. That ma-
Ma cow who cools her thin blond ankles in
A shiny ditch? Her baby's bones hurt—it's
The newness. Poplars, too, they have their secrets
With each other. Seen them at it in my
Rearview, whisperin where the smoke trees get to
Once the mist's burnt off. Why, I was in a
'Nother country by the time I knew, myself,
Where I live comfortably, to this day,
She ended, without question.

Revisionary Instruments   II

A bird I can't see outside my window is chipping away at his morning routine and mine.

And there are birds with lesser voices than his insisting on some distance, as in a child's drawing of telephone poles in which perspective is the lesson learned and wondered at.

And although it is late August, the birch next door already drops its little golden epaulets into our neighbor's garden.

They have lost a child—a three-month foetus, absorbed into the woman's body like vermin under housewalls when the lights go on.

I am tired of the deaths of the body: of the cancer that eats my friend thin, of the trout-arcing randomness and silence of it, its terrible unstillness.

There Are Plenty of Angels, She Said in the LADIES,

in the rest area LADIES on the road to
Terre Haute. Plenty of angels, *she said again.*
But not one, I've heard, not a single one
will mission to the fade as it does to the darkness.
A stall door latched. Her bag got hung.
Seen that sign back west a ways?
The one on the warehouse, in a movie marquee?
Blessed Hope, it says. Blessed Hope, *she said.*
It's meant to be a sign from heaven,
but hope's, I'd say, more a human invention,
like freeways, *she said.* Funny word—
they call em highways when you pay to ride em.
Mama's buried off one in Missouri. Had her
forty years and forty days on earth.
And the day we did it was a noisy day,
all out-o-doors like a day at the beach:
the tearin down sounds of the sun and the wind,
clouds and trees, grass and stones,
a noticeably notice-me-I'm-nature
nature sound. Mother never did care much
for nature. Enjoyed a sunset well enough.
Those shameless ones like colored candy,
those ones can look like wall-to-wall
in a cineplex foyer: pinks and purples, reds,
she said. It was so noisy, anyway,
that day even the birds shut up for once.
Or got their singin drownded out.
But I could hear when the box hit bottom:
Get on with it, is what it sounded like to me—
she had dried her hands on a paper towel—
I'm done here.

44

Revisionary Instruments   III

The beagle out back barks with a hound's voice, barks with a seal's voice, that hoarse and fish-hungry.

Her owners let rooms in a shingled house, leave rarely, are never idle.

Even their boys, jostling each other on the seat of a mower, manage, anyhow, to look purposeful.

They travel the lengths of the sidewalks and alleys they've been ordered to stay on, and do; shouting above the engine sounds, scattering squirrels to the borders.

How cleanly Paradise contains them this way. How well they guard it on their noisy rounds.

And when squirrels wheel up the charred trunks of the birch on their circus feet, in their Fred Astaire shoes, to where are they riding? What do they see?

There are rows of slate rooftops beyond this roof; there are staves of black cables collapsing to one;

and the grids made by lawn and the grids made by street ease out toward the fields leaning back into meadow:

grasses and goldenrod wind-pressed and groomed, parted and smoothed like the hair on a child.

Beyond, the woods barely hold in the river, being tugged by the river as it comes and goes by.

On its jagged teeth, past its rusted keys, it's a long roll of music, running down.

She Attempts to Tell the Truth about True Romance

Don't know a man or woman can do it, tell the truth about love.

Don't know a man or woman that knows it.

One look at the popularity o them books and magazines on the subject where the only place a woman sweats s'between her bosoms and even the saddest endin's meant to make us swoon shows that

ploppin real boys and girls down in the middle o that makes for a different story altogether and that's cause enough for their existin in the first place.

And while most grownups realize that, they ain't heartily resigned,

creatin swarms o young people ill prepared for disappointment and one mightily vicious circle I might add.

And Michael and I was afraid at the end of August.

It's only now I know how's afraid we were.

We'd heard a lot about love but nothin useful,

the usual jabber bout reputation when it's peace of mind advice was called for, tips on savin some of our sanity's opposed to virginity.

But since when's a parent done anythin right when it comes to the love of a child, and if they did Cupid's mama'd a slapped that bow and arrow right outa her son's hand when she had a chance and placed a .45 in his chubby fist instead.

Least that way we'd be sooner dead.

But I digress.

See I saw a boy on the bus just today toss the hair off his face like a bad memory,

with a quick lil jerk o his head to the right like Michael used to do,

or I mightn't a gotten on the topic at all.

Yes he'd the name o the archangel alright which made me happy at the time and disposed me toward him—

I was that kinda girl—

and he and I's fallin deep that August which is where the fright came from,

and it's a sick joke on us that the commonest occurrences such as this, birth, and death don't get related proper but I'll try my best which is more 'an most as I've already said.

Michael claimed he knew where the deer slept that summer and not half believin I followed him there,

just a giant nest o pine needles and dry leaves in a clearin in the woods of which he smelled,

and there was antler fuzz flyin everwhere from the teenagers scrapin their new horny growth off.

Saw it clingin myself to the treebark and boulders like milkweed or cottonwood or dandelions only velveter—

Michael filled my hands with it—

and I remarked how it must hurt though they's compelled to do it and don't all livin creatures know a thing about that,

where's Michael said it more involved a markin as in territories: cat glands, dog piss, creasin the corner of a book page down to find your place,

just so much more o that here-I-am, remember-me, here-you-are, so-once-was-I,

and then he pointed at a hole fresh-dug, some stones around it, and told me he'd buried some split wood there, half-charred he'd found the day we'd met,

and that in time the earth like a hidden furnace'd turn the wood to coal and the coal to diamond which he'd be placin on the third finger of my right hand in a life to come.

A life to come.

Had himself his spiritual side that boy even with both his hands down my pants.

And when it comes to romance I've not met a man since to compare.

Rain and bicycles got married in my mind.

He'd had one that summer and i'd been a wet one, and my how he sounded like rain when he came and rain when he rode away.

And when I told him so as I did each time he'd say "Then kiss the drizzle of me, darlin" and laugh so's his gums showed and what could I do?—

my body vibratin like a dozen violins backed into a corner.

We'd pile a stack o records on the phonograph and rock on the porch swing til our backs held the rhythm of it,

even off the swing and parted—

why I swung in my sleep!—

and just about when the last record spun out sayin dusk dusk there'd be suddenly sundown in earnest,

Michael's forearms blazin like the peaches he ate and my face lit up like there was sunset in my own skull.

And I've related already his hair tossin gesture and the thing with his gums and his two magic tricks—

did I tell you those?—

but mostly I loved how he'd look at me, that summer, like there wasn't as much longin in the world as in his heart,

and it was just about when that look ended,

got inexplicably tossed off his face like his too-long hair, and the one where I felt like a dull lesson in a schoolbook begun,

that I started wishin he'd just be shot clean through the chest one day so's I could mourn beautiful like Maria,

and swear truthful I'd been loved right that one time,

and have done with it.

Course if wishes were horses we'd all ride to town.

And truth be known that Frenchman was right: "The heart changes and that is our worst misfortune."

And askin why's bout as useful as askin why anythin does—slow and sneaky-like so you don't take notice.

Guess any time that dyin takes is slow.

And when it comes to love it don't go pretty like autumn or the end of a day. T'ain't a song that plays but regretful music nonetheless,

an aria o exclamation on out into eternity where the coal turns to diamonds and the deer-down you hold in the round of your arms is so light it's like the shape of a loneliness.

Grief so much everywhere you hardly notice anymore. Like that last record left over-long on the phonograph, it's in people's hearts,

and it goes Tsk.
Tsk Tsk.
Tsk Tsk.
Tsk Tsk. . . .

Revisionary Instruments   IV

Two children lean over a puzzle of wildflowers and work their way in
from the edges.

Already the foreground's made whole enough to see some shavings of
noon sun glint above the asters,

as it does in the girl's amazing hair,

which is soft and sparrow-colored closest to her skull, flecked goldly
and roped where the summer's found it.

For awhile, uncowed by the waiting room calm, they passed the box-
top model between them; they fingered the unattached pieces like pros;

but now the boy is sunk in his seat, the small girl climbs their mother's
lap, and I wonder which one of her children is sick.

In his portrait of Hart Crane, David Àlfaro Siqueiros painted the poet's
eyes closed: too much pain in them, he said.

Of whose pain, really, do the shut eyes speak? And what is one to do,
then, with this mother's pain:

her own eyes cast across the room, fixed on nothing, filled with what?

What does it look like, after all, Siqueiros? Mr. Crane, how does it
sound?

In the smudge-pots glowing through a blackened orchard, one sees it;
in the sideways trot of a highway dog.

And in the call of the fog horn, owl, and train, which is the trinity of longing in un-human throats;

in our throats, one hears it;

and in phones rung slammed, and in lamps switched off, and in blood fresh-drawn and the shit-smeared sheets,

in the headlights' reach and our lovers', too, thrum the *I would* s . . . *if you'd* s . . . *only* s . . . *give me* s . . .

of the deals wanting daily to be struck. They may not get made.

And the jigsaws spread on their low-slung tables aren't willing themselves, as we'd hoped, into shape.

It's this hopefulness some eyes go past, that is not despair, but a keener grief. In her brown eyes it is clear and deep, and is hardly there, and is all she is.

When the clerk calls from the patient list, it is she who pushes her child to the floor, kisses her hair, disappears through the door.

Her Advice to the
Still Life Painter

Limes.
Three limes or
three peeled kiwi maybe but
not grapes.
To get proper grapes you've got to
breathe on them some,
fog em up, thin the skins.
There's something dark at the heart of a grape,
like a lake that way or the unborn's eyes.
And I don't mean to criticize but
dim-lit, son,
is how grapes are,
like ice that don't reflect no more—
snowy, thick old, hoary ice:
"To hoary age I shall bear you on.
I have made you and I shall sustain you. . . ."
Bible, you know.
No? So, no. You go and
scrub grapes, skin grapes, polish grapes, or buff grapes—
they'll still end up more pearls 'an diamonds.
And what you have here, young man,
is diamonds: pure and simple,
tough and shiny, ever and all manner of light inside.
And you don't want that. Now,
who does? You want pearls? You want
grapes? What you want can roll. What you want can hide.

Revisionary Instruments   V

Another August, midday clouds, a wind with autumn in its mouth, craw full of rain.

The psychic maple leaves predict it, a-flex and fluttering in one-handed applause.

And when it falls the sound it makes is less and more than falling rain:

a bicycle that comes and goes, a blown leaf skipping up the street—how oddly drier than itself! Chameleon rain, protean bicycle.

And if I am waiting, ticking time like the leaves, and if I am grieving, thick and sure as the rain, as the draping rain, is it not too soon?

> *Too soon*, calls a bird.

Is it not too late?

> *Too late, too late.*

> It's perched inside your husband's eye
> (I saw it in a dream last night).
> It looks as if it means to stay
> (I held his face up to the light).
> And doesn't budge, and doesn't sing,
> And will not tell me anything.

> It is much too late to tell me now.

Her Meditation on the Subject of Universal Phenomena

Havin been accused o shapin experience to suit my will,
as no doubt you at times have done, I'm devotin one
entire season to a study o the new physics.

This book here my librarian swears is most highly readable,

and when I ask him why's I shouldn't begin with th'old
physics first he don't crack a smile but tells me it's best
to stay current while one can which I very much liked
and winked at him for.

I admire reserve and humor more. And I'm havin to exhibit
quantities o both on this venture.

Too much truth's a one-way teacher, it's fiction makes
the better friend. Still it hurts me some what I ain't got
reasons for.

How them pines f'rinstance stand up in wind when one good
rain'll lay peonies flat, pink and pinker like bridesmaids in a heap,
ashes ashes fallin down.

Horrible rhyme. The worse the better for children which is a
'nother mystery this text prob'ly don't address.

My only daughter, whom I name Rose cause she come out
that blue some red roses got on em, sung it,

later o course when she cleared up and got so sweet my teeth
hurt to watch her so I call her Sugar and that sorta stuck:

Sugar Rose, Sugar Rose, like those ones you scrape to the side
o your cakeplate.

Then she turn thirteen, all that uppity baby-birded wide-
openness gone from her, and dub herself Francie—

after the country she says though more likely for a older girl
she love and which I tried respectin but backfired on her
Papa who called her Rose, Sugar Rose, nor Francie then neither
but Fancy Pants.

He's mean those days when he waren't keepin to hisself.
Belly soundin like a haunted house, he pled gastric dis-
tress but his head too were off.

I caught him buttonin a hangin shirt o his one day like there's
somebody in it required protectin. Then he told me the cat needed
groundin, as in electrically. Said the cat should be electrically
grounded and he'd hatched a plan to do it.

A river were always colder with that man in it, leastways
in latter times.

And when he left us I's turnin paired critters outa our house
like Noah in reverse: Mr. and Mrs. Cricket, Sparrow, Beetle
and Bottlefly, just life imitatin life and a late omen if ever
I seen one.

Lupine in the sideyard had its jets turned low right then
and calla lilies the neighbor lady grew on sticks didn't look
like things the world had made.

And I begun considerin th'elements and seasons and our
very own natures,

which commenced with a colonial bed lamp I'd neglected
dustin and which I'd inherited from Mama, a white porcelain

with pimples arrangement and a shade with eagles spread-
eagled o'er declarations o independence.

Believed she shoulda been New England gentry, my Mama,
and hers afore her couldn't soak enough sun like she's born
off the coast o Spain or somethin which she was not.

You don't think you'll end up here nor there but wind up
somewhere anyhow til you realize it's the wrong place
and has been all along.

And I think heaven if there is any justice would simply be
gettin born to what's true for us, a sorta spiritual Denmark
where a soul could choose, like Rose did with Francie
which was little but somethin.

And for those of us who ain't got strong leanins, well,
we could just rest, traditional-like.

Look,

this fire here's all exits. And rain, see, it finds its way
down. And together they makes a stitchin o what they are
like twin clocks identical ever way exceptin one says six
and th'other half past twelve,

kind of a two-lane highway goin not north nor south exactly
but high and deep if y'all can imagine it. Verticality's enough
to get you vertigone.

I myself prefer sweepin the latitudes these days, the side-
by-sides, the cheek-to-cheeks. It's a priv'lege o age and th'only
one as I can see.

A crab mostly gets where it's goin now don't it? The soft shell
suit me fine.

Revisionary Instruments   VI

I don't know where to go from here. We can admit that now.

I wanted to write a poem so true our hearts would ring and tilt into the dip of it.

Let us forget that now.

For the waiting is over, and the poem I thought so nearly finished, not the one I had in mind.

What hand will it hold now, after all? What blood give? or breath? Nor can it help the dying into death.

I thought to write, and wrote it once:

The steam from some utility that pours along the walk, that breaks in waves and eddies round our shins, belongs to us.

And grackles in the tallest trees—those black coiffures, that raucous noise

tossed down like bread on to the path we cut—we own them too.

But never had it seemed that way: that we possessed and were possessed,

like film snagged on a single frame with our scene held suspended there,

as if some mad projectionist said, *Here's a bite of memory for you. Go and chew on this awhile.*

No. At best, my friend, it was a show, like all the rest,

of lost keys and tiny miracles, which we attended casually. How could
we do otherwise?

Yet I remember so much:

the turning leaves you loved, the sureness of your stride, your voice,
your hands,

and the cherries you purchased, so dear at that season,

which you fed to the birds, sleek-throated and black, who flung the
stones behind their backs, and begged for more.

Triptych

I *OTHERWISE*

Gooseneck loosestrife,
              yarrow in a garden, and
starlings spread-eagle
                on a back lawn in the sun.
Having glutted themselves
              all morning
                    on mulberries,
beneath them the grass
             must feel cool as they rest.
                        But at first
she'd been alarmed,
           stepping from her bath,
                  to see them so
motionless, wrenched wing-wide
                as if dead,
    and it took some mother in her—
Just a dream sweet
           nothing in the closet dear
heart—to assure her otherwise.

Late afternoon,
pleasure boats in the river
                    bob whitely, serenely,
both the tethered and the manned.
                            And sunlight flares
up scales on the current,
            pizzicato,
                        like memory and its faux-jewel tones.
Walking here one day last winter,
                        sky blank with unfallen snow,
a friend told sadly a story she'd read
                        of a man in love
with a phantom mate:
                his ideal lover, the adult
                                extension
        of a lonely child's imaginary friend.
This afternoon,
            though she recalls neither
                            the story's title
            nor cause of that
woman's particular sorrow—the swallowed
        keening, her shadowed
                        face—phrases
her dead friend made do
                return,
                    like *blueprints*
        for love, self-
                authored perfection;
        and the question
she'd asked,
            in a thicker voice,
                    which was *Why*
    do you think we remain
            so lonesome,

if forever, in a sense,
we accompany ourselves?
Snowfall had muffled their footsteps by then,

and river fog

rising within its banks

became a river

detached from its source,

like the visible

breaths the women let go of

along with their words

in the winter air.

III *NO MESSAGE*

Tents of after-rain in suburban trees,
mist on the macadam, and
a sycamore's wanness under the moon put
specters on the face of things,
or so she thinks as she waits on the porch,
minding the night like a house in her charge.
And when figures advance from the end
of her street, darkly
clothed, luminously tracking
as the storm had tracked,
she is not surprised;
she is ready for the visit
of these wraiths, and their answer;
she is eager (they would know it)
for the message they bring.
So what, then, whose mercy, whose
failure, or idea of
the real dissolves them as wholly
as they'd just appeared,
and makes them trees and white
siding again, and leaves
no message but the last
leaf-rain, headlights
rounding the corner they'd stood on, all things,
things as they apparently are.